FROM DISTRESS TO DE-STRESS

FINDING PEACE WITHIN

DR. MILIND HARI PATWARDHAN

ISBN 979-888521027-0

This book is dedicated to
Dr. Hans Selye, (father of stressollogy)
& Dr. Martin Seligman (father of positive psychology)

Contents

Foreword *vii*

Preface *ix*

Preface Ii *xi*

1. Talking About Stress 1
2. What Is Stress Response System? 8
3. Stress - Management 14
4. Breathing Exercises For Relaxation 23
5. Autogenic Training For Reducing Anxiety 28
6. How To Begin A Basic Meditation Practice? 35
7. Mindfulness 42
8. Polyvagal Theory - Importance Of Vagus Nerve 56
9. Cognitive Behavioural Therapy (cbt) 66

Epilogue 71

About The Author 73

Foreword

In the last 100 years, with the help of technological advances, the average longevity of man has increased by 30 years or so. We are living longer but not healthier lives.

The everyday stress of living is producing an alteration in our internal milieu; which is favouring explosive increases in many chronic diseases. In fact, science has proved that many diseases like obesity, metabolic syndrome, diabetes, dementia, atherosclerosis, ischemic heart disease, hypertension, depression, failing immune system, certain gastric & intestinal disturbances, cancers, arthritis, and many of our modern plagues can be linked to our stressful lifestyle.

At the same time, behavioural scientists are proving that the common, everyday stress is mainly in the "perception" of the individual. No two subjects exposed to the same stressful situations will have the same reactions and consequences. Extensive research on stress response has revealed the major role the endocrine system plays in evoking Stress Response. With more understanding of neurobiology, now we are exploring how to invoke Relaxation Response. To change our self-sabotaging & destructive behaviour in response to an actual or imagined threat, we have to examine our beliefs, our conditioning & our reflex, impulsive thought patterns.

Apart from CBT (Cognitive Behavioural Therapy) as a psychoanalytical process, Meditation, Mindfulness Meditation, Visualization, Vipassana, Progressive Muscular Relaxation and Deep abdominal slow breathing, Qui gong & Yoga Acupressure, Massage & Music Therapy are also being investigated in clinical settings. It is the need of the hour that we recognize our stressors & build on our resources to build Resilience. If we do this, we will create a happy and healthy society, rather than just a long-living but frustrated, crippled, diseased, and purposeless mass of lost humanity.

Yes, it is historical time. If we do not change ourselves now, our future generations will be most ungrateful to us for our selfish, short-sighted, and negligent behavior, which we are handing them down as a legacy. If we change ourselves, we will have changed our world that bit at least, right? This book is an attempt to bring the latest knowledge about stress & its pathophysiology as well as research that explores how we can reduce stress and its effects on our life. I have summarised some of the common techniques advocated for stress management.

A word of caution: most of the exercises used as stress relievers work no doubt immediately, but repeatedly doing them as a lifelong habit is important to combat the side-effects of chronic stress. These exercises work very well & are found to be more effective when used with Cognitive & Behavioural modifications. These combined therapies are as effective as drugs, but an expert opinion is always required, advisable & should not be avoided.

This book is not meant to replace proper medical advice.

I hope this book motivates you for further action. Doctors are found to be very susceptible to stress-induced burnout. So this is one way to help my colleagues to avoid it. I can not but express my sincere thanks to the cooperation of my wife Dr. Varsha, who allowed me the luxury of all the available time to study to write, rewrite & proofread & re-read, without which this book wouldn't have seen the light of the day.

I am thankful to my daughter, Dr.Ketaki Patwardhan (Nirkhi), for helping me with the editing and this edition and designing the cover. Many of my friends have helped me, through discussions and chats, to formulate my ideas. I am overwhelmed by their love & support.

I am thankful to Dr. Mrs. Vaishali Deshmukh & Dr. Vishwnath Magdum, for writing the preface.

Dr Milind H Patwardhan.
ENDOCRINOLOGIST, Miraj

Preface

"From Distress to De-stress": A book written by Dr. Milind Patwardhan is an excellent new addition to know everything regarding stress and its management.

The modern medicine has made tremendous progress in treating diseases of the body, but has neglected the mind. We have to understand that the body and the mind are not separate entities, and one affects the other every moment, which means, a healthy mind can lead to a healthy body and vice-versa. Our forefathers knew this long back and even the Western world recognized it before us, but we have not bothered to give attention to it. With modern lifestyle, stress has become an inevitable part of life, but we have failed to overcome it and the consequences of this are many diseases, like hypertension, heart disease, diabetes, obesity, depression, cancer, etc which are rampant.

This epidemic of non-communicable diseases is making havoc in our society. Just treating them with modern medicine is not going to be beneficial, but we have to find ways to prevent them. This book is one step in that direction.

Dr. Milind Patvardhan is the first Endocrinologist in Western Maharashtra, practicing and training medical fraternity for the last 40 years. His efforts to make society aware of how diabetes can be controlled through lifestyle changes, how to avoid complications of this chronic lifelong malady through books, magazines, lectures & patient education camps are highly appreciated.

Dr. Patwardhan has profound knowledge of spirituality as well as modern psychology. So, how ancient philosophy and modern medicine can be combined and utilized for the betterment of mankind is very lucidly and authentically explained by him in this book. How stress is caused, its pathophysiology, and its effects on various body systems are explained in detail. Stress is part of modern life and is essential for development and progress but if our response to chronic stress is often not proper. It can lead to deleterious effects on various systems of the body. They are preventable to a large extent.

The topic on meditation is a masterstroke: what is meditation, how it helps us to overcome stress, different types of meditation, and practical tips to make meditation a part of our routine life is explained in a simple yet effective manner.

Presently we are fighting Covid Pandemic and living in the Covid era, where there is fear, uncertainty, and anxiety is a challenge faced by everybody. This is the time when stress management is very important. During this stressful period, this book is a gift to all of us. I am sure what you are holding in your hands right now can be a life-saving message, maybe for you or your family members or your friends

Dr. Vishwanath N. Magdum,
Urologist, Kolhapur.

Preface Ii

Every bodily act and disease is controlled by the mind, as mind and body are the two sides of the same coin, and are thus inseparable. Hence one is known to influence the other significantly, which means that only a healthy mind can lead to a healthy body and vice versa. In spite of technical advances and improvement in socioeconomic conditions, nutrition, exercise, fitness, health awareness and newer drugs, there is a rapid increase in the prevalence of all non-communicable diseases like diabetes, hypertension, heart disease, depression and cancers. The reason for this probably lies in the deteriorating mental health of the people over the past few decades. Hence the need to improve mental health and pay specific attention to the mind as we do to our bodies.

Mind health and MBM (Mind body Medicine) have origins and roots in traditional and age-old Indian health practices. However, the irony of the situation is that MBM has more efficiently been practiced along with Modern Medicine outside India. This book attempts to give key learnings to all the readers to use MBM practice in their routine, to help patients and the common man in general. Stress response, which is nature's way to combat stress, was initially useful to cavemen to improve survival. The archetypal stress response of our ancestors was classically FIGHT/FLIGHT or FREEZE response to threat, which helped them to survive all odds of nature. But with time it is now being activated in response to social, cultural, financial and even imaginary threats.

For ages, beginning from the era of Buddha, people have been in search of peace & happiness which are antidotes to stress. This book has been written by Dr. Milind Patwardhan, an eminent and senior endocrinologist from Miraj, India, as an attempt to ease the understanding of the phenomenon of stress and how to de-stress oneself as a doctor and as an individual.

Dr. Milind Patwardhan, who also happens to be the first qualified Endocrinologist from Maharashtra, India, has amassed great clinical wisdom in his 35 years of practice & has distilled his learning for all of us. I wish this project every success & am sure readers are going to read this manual on stress management again & again.

Dr (Mrs) Vaishali Deshmukh
Endocrinologist, Pune

CHAPTER ONE

Talking about Stress

Human beings are surviving, thriving & flourishing on this planet Earth, for more than five million years. During the course of evolution, we have developed a very efficient survival system.

This system constantly keeps scanning our environment and if it senses a threat, a danger to life; in the form of an enemy or a predator, then it immediately activates life-preserving reflex activity, commonly known as the Stress Response. It prepares us for the fight, or flight - either face the devil or run away. Once we are back in a safe environment again, the stress response subsides and we relax, rest, feed & breed.

So we have survived - not only survived but thrived. We are flourishing and now we have created safety around us. We no longer face an enemy or a predator as was faced by our ancestors.

But still, our stress response is activated. This activation is a result of various triggers, which are now the modern-day enemies or predators.

If your boss threatens you, your wife/spouse starts a fight or some major life event (e.g. marriage, divorce, death of a kin, etc.) occurs, you feel threatened. Your self-image, your 'ego' feels threatened. Your brain & your body, not knowing how to deal with this, activates your stress response. This can be activated even by your imaginations and memories.

The response which our body produces to a stressor is either adequate or inadequate. If it is inadequate then we feel stressed out. We know that the health of the body influences the mind and in return, the health of the mind affects the body. When one feels that he/she can not cope with the demands of life, he/she feels inadequate.

This particular feeling of inadequacy or incompetency to face the challenges posed by life is termed **Stress.**

As such, Stress is a very loose term & though much abused, it is easily understood by the general public. When we suffer from an injury or from, say, a burn, or an accident or an infection causing fever, or when we undergo an operation, we are suffering from physical & physiological stress. These have been extensively studied. We also suffer psychologically, say in a competitive atmosphere, or through social discrimination & injustices, or through an unhealthy work atmosphere. We suffer because of losses, deceit, breach of trust, addiction in a family member, or when we are the sole parent or sole caretaker of our aged & diseased relative.

Presently, for the last 2 years, we are all facing the CORONA pandemic, lockdowns, untimely deaths of our family members or friends. Many have lost their jobs, earnings and are incurring losses. Children are deprived of schooling, gatherings, and social interactions. We are all facing a lot of psychological stress because of this situation. Investigations of physical and physiological stress have helped us to understand the effects of stress. It is difficult to measure psychological stress, but we can get a fair idea of the severity of stress by mapping patients' subjective perception about a stressful event on a scale prepared by psychologists or by investigating his blood sample say for measuring changes occurring in stress hormones like cortisol & adrenaline.

The problem with psychological stress is that its preception is highly dependent on the subject who is experiencing or perceiving the stressful event. The same stressful stimulus/event can evoke different reactions from different subjects. Stress being such a subjective phenomenon, it is difficult to grade it.

Scientists say that our brain churns out about 50 - 60 thousand thoughts every day, out of which, on an average, 50 to 60 carry significant stressor potentials. So habitually thinking negative thoughts, ruminating about the worse outcomes in any scenario, can produce a state of chronic stress.

Psychiatrists & psychologists don't rely on getting laboratory results to decide if you are stressed or not. They have a rating scale based on your answers to standard questionnaires that helps them to look at the level of your subjective feeling of stress and then, using the same scale, they decide whether you are improving or not. In the evaluation of the mental state, a well-documented mental status examination over a period of time is the gold standard. Cortisol, CRH (Corticotropin releasing hormone), Adrenaline are some of the hormones secreted by your endocrine system into the blood as a part of body's response to stress.

As it is, in institutional set ups, presently salivary cortisol & hair cortisol are used as markers of acute & chronic stress, respectively. Salivary cortisol correlates with serum levels of free cortisol, while hair cortisol correlates with the average cortisol levels. Hair grows at the rate of 1cm/month. Just one centimeter of hair shows the average cortisol over a month. Many stress response inventories (SRI), that is questionnaires, have been developed, which include emotional, somatic, cognitive (thinking) and behavioural stress responses, and use them to scale the stressfulness of a given life situation.

We know that those who have a high-stress score, using such inventories, if continue to have such stress chronically, are prone to develop major physical illness in 12 to 24 months. Their chances of having a stress related disorder are 50% higher than when compared to those with low stress score. Biochemical measures of stress such as heart rate variability, serum cortisol levels and inflammatory markers have been used in some research work assessing the impact of stress management interventions.

Functional neuroimaging using brain mapping to assess activities of specific areas of brain has also been used. So now that you have got an idea of what we are talking about, let us try to define Stress.

"Stress is a perceived inability to cope up with a survival threat of either an actual or an imagined stressor".

We understand that it is the individual's interpretation of a situation that will decide the severity of any given stressor event.

When stress is mild we call it a 'Challenge' or 'good stress (Eustress), but when the stress is too much, or it is producing a lot of anxiety, depression, a feeling of being paralysed by the situation, we call it 'bad stress' (Distress). Good stress motivates us into action while distress paralyzes us from any meaningful action. After all, stress is stress and at any point the Eustress can become overwhelming, demanding, depleting & turn into Distress.

In the mild to moderate category, it is euphoric arousal, helping the subject to cope up with stress. Good stress helps you to perform better, while bad stress causes your performance to deteriorate.

Stress is caused by important significant life events.

Therefore, the so-called good life events should also be considered as 'Stressors'. Just as the death of a family member is stressful, so is the birth of a new member into the family. Just as divorce is stressful, so is marriage. The Holmes Rahe stress inventory is commonly used to score your life stress. I suggest we should all undertake this inventory to know how stress-prone or stress-hardy we are. It is like know thyself. (Ref. : Frontiers in Psychology. 2015 Dec; 6: 1481. Brief quiet ego contemplation reduces oxidative stress and mind-wandering.)

Categories of Stressors

Major life events, like the death of a near relative, the birth of a child, divorce as well as marriage, getting hired for work or fired from work, changing house or town, getting framed as a criminal, retiring, any major illness, etc are all stressors & have been allocated certain marks/scores.

This is understandable. (Holmes & Rahe 1967) But major life events are rare. Day to day hassles of life also constitute added burden to the stress by their low intensity but high-frequency occurrence (Lazarus 1988); (eg. Paying bills, going shopping, time constraints, deadlines, missing a bus, etc.) These daily hassles have a hassle score which also correlates with the poor health of the victims.

Work-Related Stress :

Most of us spend more time in our work, our profession. The work atmosphere can be encouraging or discouraging. Sexual harassment, mental harassment, work overload, discrimination, unhealthy competitions, boredom all can be very stressful.

Even our children are not free from this stress. In school or playgrounds, getting bullied by others, competitive nature of examinations, too much academic workload, expectations of parents, teachers, etc. all are quite stressful.

In short in all fields of life, all ages & at all stages we are experiencing a unique mental atmosphere infected by 'Stress' virus & it is damaging to our health. In fact, stress is directly related to all the diseases which are on the rise in our educated, advanced, hi-tech & so-called cultured society.

Thus, if we do not wake up to this challenge, we & our future generations are going to be the most unhealthy humans who ever populated mother earth.

The ABC of understanding stress

A is a stressor (an event that provokes stress response), B is a person exposed to the stress & C is his/her reaction. A can be an exam, an interview, or a difficult diagnosis given to you by your doctor. C is your reaction - its physiological, psychological, immunological, and metabolic effects. B is the key deciding factor as to how you will respond & what effects you will see later on.

Animals subjected to different stressors respond by acute stress response activated through the stress system (We will discuss components of the stress system, how it works etc a little later). When the stressor subsides, the acute response in animals subsides in 90 seconds, including hormonal activation. But in humans, there is no predictability of how much time the stress response will continue even after the stressor is removed because humans can ruminate, think about it & keep the stressors active in their minds. This repetitive thinking and ruminating leads to episodic acute stress, followed eventually by chronic stress. This is followed by post-traumatic stress disorder. We, humans, have missed (how to allow the body's responses to settle down when the stressor is removed) & messed up (by brooding, negative thinking, ruminating about it automatically or habitually for a prolonged period of time) a lot.

If the person recognizes that his reaction is detrimental to his health, he can become ready for introspection. He may want to avoid stressor or minimize it, change it or exchange it, but soon he accepts that what he can change is his perception, his thinking & his behaviour.

Stress as such is an arousal signal. It is telling you 'come on, get up, be awake, come in the present moment, now & here.' One of my friends said to me once, *"I have come to a conclusion that self-realization and self-talking, and being compassionate and patient to your own self is the key to reduce underlying stress"*.

Yes, my friends, we are too critical, judgemental & harsh with ourselves. We have to dig deep inside our minds. Why do we behave the way we behave? Our behaviour, thinking patterns are determined not only by genetic, but epigenetic effects of our upbringing and conditioning. These are the most prominent factors. They are learned by age 6 to 7 yrs. They are unquestioned beliefs, useful for immediate reflex survival mode, but in many other situations, they are inadequate & inappropriate. We have not examined them. Many are unspoken to us as well.

Comparison, a feeling of superiority or inferiority & accepted definitions of success produce much stress in us. If this is brought to light we can avoid self-sabotage which we consent to without questioning.

We have to accept ourselves, love ourselves, forgive ourself & be ready to change for our better versions to come into existence.

There is a highly critical voice - a judge - a boss - sitting inside our heads. It is constantly talking, chattering. It is the voice of our conditionings, of our parents, teachers, voice of our society, our core beliefs. We feel it is our voice, it is our thoughts, but it is constantly changing its opinions, it talks for and against any issue. It tries to dominate us. It can literally turn us mad.

This brings us to the role of CBD - Cognitive Behavioural Therapy and MBSR programs (i.e Mindfulness Based Stress Reduction program) in educating us about how to manage our stress. But before that, I think we will examine the stress system, stress response, chronic stress, and its contribution to chronic diseases.

We are all creations of the creator who forgot to provide us with a user manual with this body-mind apparatus. But probably that is the game. Find yourself and you are at ease with all creation. Life is full of wonders and we will find ourselves grateful for this beautiful journey.

CHAPTER TWO

What is stress Response System?

One Mind, Three Brains (Triune Brain)

As we evolved, our brains also evolved. Our Reptilian brain was acquired first. It is in charge of our primal instincts. Then we evolved to acquire the Limbic Brain, our emotional brain & lastly we evolved into frontal & pre-frontal Brain (Neo Cortex), our rational, thinking Brain (Mac Lean's Model). When we are in danger & must respond quickly, as an act of self-preservation, the reptilian structure is aroused, preparing us for fight or flight. (The Stress response).

When we hear a piece of good or bad news, we are emotionally activated because our Limbic system gets involved. When we are solving a problem, thinking logically, our neocortex is engaged. Coming to stress response, it is under the control of our Reptilian Brain. It consists of Amygdala, its sensory connections & dopaminergic projections.

Amygdala is the sentry, to watch over the environment and scan for any threat or danger signal. It receives all sensory input, and also projections from the midbrain and the brainstem, which store aversion-producing memories. These (external signals + internal reference memories) are further presented to the basolateral nucleus in Amygdala to scan this data, to decide the stressor potential of the situation.

The basolateral Nucleus processes this, decides severity to take a decision, and projects effector (dopaminergic) signals to the Nucleus Ceruleus. This all happens in just microseconds. Amygdala is the emotional brain. It has access to negative memories & negative emotions stored in the hippocampus. If the incoming signal matches any previous negative memory, Amygdala literally hijacks the response and activates the stress response. This activates two arms of the stress response. One is the CRH arm and the other is the central sympathetic response.

So you see, the Amygdala, through evolution, has become a fantastic instrument to scan threat, danger, or negativity. It is basically meant for this. So we are all extremely efficient to pick up negative signals, we ignore all good, safe & positive signals.

We have to start re-training ourselves from this step. To pick up negativity, to search for danger & potentially threatful situations is the body's normal, natural protective reflex. But now, you are not in any physical danger most of the times.

So you have to activate & train yourself to pick up the positive signals in your surroundings. Start noticing what is positive in your life. Every day, find three positive things for which you should be grateful to the cosmos. Keep a journal. Slowly, with regular practice, you will start to find and focus on the positive aspects of life. This is a small but important step to reduce impulsive negative focus.

The two arms of Stress response.

What are these two arms of the endocrine stress response, how do they positively or negatively give feedback on each other & what are the natural balancing systems to bring back the stress response to a normal homeostatic state? (This process is called Allotasis).

The hypothalamus is a bit like a command center. This area of the brain communicates with the rest of the body through the autonomic nervous system, which controls such involuntary body functions as breathing, blood pressure, heartbeat, and the dilatation or constriction of the key blood vessels and small airways in the lungs (bronchioles).

The autonomic nervous system has two components, the sympathetic nervous system, and the parasympathetic nervous system. The sympathetic nervous system functions like an accelerator pedal in a car. It triggers the fight-or-flight response, (that is, the body immediately prepares either for fighting with the threatening challenge or if it feels safer to run, it prepares to run away from this threat). This requires a lot of energy to be made available. The body has to be provided with a burst of energy so that it can respond to perceived dangers.

The parasympathetic nervous system acts like a brake. It promotes the "rest and digest" response that calms the body down after the danger has passed. After the amygdala sends a distress signal, the hypothalamus activates the sympathetic nervous system by sending signals through the autonomic nerves to the adrenal glands. These glands respond by pumping the hormone epinephrine (also known as adrenaline) into the bloodstream.

As epinephrine circulates through the body, it brings on a number of physiological changes. The heart beats faster than normal, pushing blood to the muscles, heart, and other vital organs. Pulse rate and blood pressure go up. The person undergoing these changes also starts to breathe more rapidly. Small airways in the lungs open wide. This way, the lungs can take in as much oxygen as possible with each breath. Extra oxygen is sent to the brain, increasing alertness. Sight, hearing, and other senses become sharper. Meanwhile, epinephrine triggers the release of blood sugar (glucose) and fats from temporary storage as a source of energy.

This is all in preparation to give instantaneous energy to the body, either to fight or to take flight. Unfortunately in today's life you can neither fight nor take flight, so you have to take the brunt of all such chronic unabated stress. The environment in which we live has got revolutionized to produce newer stressors, but the body's stress system has not evolved to cope with it, so we have to find ways to help our body & brain; to design newer connections, to offset the side effects of this overflowing chronic stress responses.

In other words, we have to find a switch for our own 'Relaxation response'.

Now please tolerate a little bit more complex explanation of an important part of the hormonal mediator of stress, Cortisol.

CRH (Corticotropin Releasing Hormone) produced by hypothalamic neurons acts on CRH - 1R (Central) & CRH2-R (peripheral) receptors. These receptors bring about behavioral & immunological changes to adapt to the threat. CRH also enters the portal system & the HPA axis is activated causing a release of stress hormone - Cortisol - which plays the most important role in Metabolic & immune adaptations.

Adrenaline is important in the immediate stress response. Cortisol also increases the sugar levels in the blood, enhances your brain's use of sugar, and also increases the availability of substances required for tissue repair. Cortisol affects responses of the immune system. The bodily functions which are not required during stress response are suppressed by cortisol. Digestive, reproductive & growth functions are thus suppressed and the energy which was being used by them can now be shunted to tissues & organs that need it the most.

How does stress produce diseases?

We saw, that when the Amygdala senses a threat to survival, it kicks the Neural & Endocrine Systems into action. But another limb activated by stress is the body's immune system. This is where Psycho-Neuro-Endocrine-Immunology (PNEI) (Pelletier 1988) comes in.

Neural Limb: Stress response activates the Neural (autonomic) limb, causing faster & forceful heartbeats, faster & shallow respiratory rate, high blood faster & shallow respiratory rate, high blood pressure, etc. Usually, these are short-lived and subside once the stressor is removed. But repeated acute or chronic unabated stress produces these reactions again & again.

This may lead to high blood pressure, heart disease, peptic ulcers, Asthma, Panic attacks (sudden feeling of impending doom, fear, anxiety, air hunger), anxiety states. When over alert, the highly sensitive Amygdala keeps on sending 'emergency' cry signals repeatedly to the limbic & autonomic nervous systems These systems can get depleted of neurotransmitters.

To save the machinery from overuse, abuse, and false alarm, the brain tries to raise the threshold of perception so that Amygdala would not respond to minor threats. But because of this increase in the threshold of perception, the brain starts missing out on positive, good, and safe new signals also.

In this way, the brain lacking positive feedback can lead to Depressive effects. In fact, this is the basis of how Depression, anxiety, and panic attacks are caused & perpetuated by chronic stress and how they can be treated by cognitive & behavioural intervention.

Endocrine Limb: Stress activates the CRH-ACTH-Cortisol axis. The resultant hypercortisolemia gives energy to muscles and the brain by Gluco-neo-genesis; it also increases the availability of substances that repair tissues. It alters responses of the immune system & suppresses the digestive, reproductive & growth systems. When you are subjected to chronic stress, you become chronically (albeit mildly) hypercortisolemic. So you become prone to obesity (especially central), develop hyperglycemia & hypertriglyceridemia, ultimately leading to Diabetes.

Immune alterations: Stress alters the body's T & B Lymphocyte's functions. Stress impairs the body's ability to fight infections. Especially chronic stress is responsible for increased viral infections (such as Influenza, Corona, Herpes, etc.) and decreased wound healing. Chronic unabated stress results in a state of chronic inflammation. Chronic inflammation is associated with Atherosclerosis, IHD, Diabetes, depression, psoriasis, Rheumatoid arthritis, etc. Immune cells are also involved in cancer surveillance.

Therefore it is not surprising that chronic stress is associated with an increase in the incidence and progression of cancers. Hypercortisolemia also negatively influences many immune functions. Antibodies of lgA class are secreted in saliva & can be measured. During stressful periods salivary IgA levels significantly decline.

CHAPTER THREE

STRESS - MANAGEMENT

What is Relaxation Response

With the availability of the internet, explosion of information on social media, and the like, the number of distractions has increased in our life. In fact, I would say this is the age of distraction. It has become easier to become less mindful, absent-minded, multi-tasking robot rather than a feeling, loving, mindfully listening, human being. Minds are constantly polluted by toxic and negative media and news. Such a mind which has lost its balance because it has no time for itself, for introspection, is very prone to distractions.

Meditation is a way to detoxify the mind from sensory bombardment, sensory overload & multitudes of daily distractions which interfere with clear thinking, and don't allow the mind a moment of peace. From time immemorial, most ancient cultures, civilizations & eastern religions have developed techniques to calm the mind, bring in serenity, & a feeling of connectedness with our source energy. This is known to reduce stress levels & get ourselves rejuvenated.

In the last nearly hundred years or so, meditation has become the password of New Age & taken the world, including the scientific & medical community, under its fold. Once thought to be esoteric, meditation now has become accepted as a non-religious, secular practice to reduce the effects of stress on the body and mind, and this has been proved time & again.

Transcendental Meditation (TM) was brought to the USA in the 1960s by Maharshi Mahesh Yogi. TM is a simplified meditation technique that has been extensively tested in laboratories (Benson & Wallance 1972). Dr. Herbert Benson, a Harvard Medical Professor, became an ardent meditator under Maharshis's guidance.

Dr. Herbert Benson argued that if the body and the brain have a mechanism to produce stress response to combat the dangers to our existence; then the body and the brain must also have a response that will decrease all the negative effects of stress & help the body to come back to homeostasis. He termed this response as Relaxation Response.

He hypothesized that if switched on, this Relaxation Response would activate the circuitry in the brain involving the parasympathetic nervous system to calm down the body activated by the sympathetic nervous system during stress.

This was logical. Dr. Benson studied the effects of TM in its participants, felt convinced about its huge benefits & brought it to the medical fraternity. He removed meditation from the shadow of religion by removing mantra, gurudiskha, etc & made it accessible to the common man. It was an instant hit.

The concept of meditation was introduced to the west in the 1900s. There is a tradition of Christian meditation - Prayer, practicing the presence of God; but that had not yet attracted medical attention. Rational thinking was the Socratarian method of confronting your demons.

The simplest & universal technique to combat stress is taking a nap, having a good night's sleep. Sleeping over the problem, so to say. But chronic continuous unresolved stress produces an unabated arousal response, leading to chronic insomnia as one of the manifestations of chronic stress. In TM, the certified teachers explained to the client about the theory part. Then he was taught deep breathing exercises. Then the teacher would find a Vedic mantra special for the client. Maharshi advised that this special Mantra should always be kept secret to be effective, (a statement later proved to be unfounded) and have him repeat it slowly during exhalation. TM sessions of twenty minutes twice a day were advised. Then a prayer was taught. Dr. Benson modified it.

The Relaxation Response is a helpful way to turn off the fight-or-flight response and bring the body back to pre-stress levels. Dr. Benson describes the Relaxation Response as a physical state of deep relaxation which engages the other part of our Autonomic nervous system - the parasympathetic nervous system.

Research has shown that regular use of the Relaxation Response can help any health problem that is caused or exacerbated by chronic stress such as fibromyalgia, gastrointestinal ailments, insomnia, hypertension, anxiety disorders, and others.

Dr. Benson demystified TM by doing away with some queer mantra. What he initially experimented with is quite interesting. He took the telephone directory & made the client select at random 2 to 3 names, then selected 1 to 2 letters from each & prepared a meaningless word to be given to the meditator as his/ her mantra & found that it also worked well.

In his book 'The Relaxation Response', Dr. Benson describes four basic steps to follow: They are

1) Aquiet Environment: Any place with minimal distractions, you should feel comfortable. The minimum the sensory input/ distractions, the better.

2) A mental Device: This is an object or tool used to replace all other thoughts. It is a focal point to which you are going to direct all your attention. A mental device can include repetition of a mantra, or focussed breathing, or a tratak or a Nadam (e.g. Tibetian bowls). Dr. Benson suggested the word 'one' as a mantra. He has also suggested that if the mind wanders, use the word 'no' to discontinue proliferation of free association.

3) A passive Attitude: This is a receptive attitude. You should be open to thoughts with awareness. Don't try to block your thoughts. If you resist, they get momentum, energy. If you just observe & come back to your focus of attention, the mantra 'one', then they drift away and disappear.

4) Comfortable Position: The body should be at ease, but avoid a position conducive to sleep. Be well supported in a straight-back chair.

There are many methods to elicit the Relaxation Response including visualization, progressive muscle relaxation, energy healing, acupuncture, massage, breathing techniques, prayer, meditation, Tai chi, Qui gong, and yoga. True relaxation can also be achieved by removing yourself from everyday thoughts by listening to a piece of soothing music, listening to a rhythmic religious chant, or visualizing a beautiful, peaceful excursion in nature.

Why did Transcendental Meditation (TM) become an instant success?

It removed you from your everyday stressful thinking & by repetition of a meaningless word, it dulled the conscious mind.

Dr. Benson says that the elicitation of relaxation response depends on two steps, these most important two steps are - one is a repetition of your mantra & the second is the ability to push aside intruding daily thoughts & come back to the mantra.

You Must Relax !! (It sounds contradictory, isn't it?)

One of the most valuable things we can do in life is to learn deep relaxation — making an effort to spend some time every day, quieting our minds, to create inner peace and better health.

Following is the Relaxation Response technique taken directly from Dr. Herbert Benson's book, The Relaxation Response.

Steps to Elicit the Relaxation Response -

- Sit quietly in a comfortable position.
- Close your eyes.
- Deeply relax all your muscles, beginning at your feet and progressing up to your face. Keep them relaxed. [Relax your tongue—and thoughts will cease.]
- Breathe through your nose. Become aware of your breathing. As you breathe out, say the word "one"* silently to yourself. For

example, breathe in, and then out, and say "one", in and out, and repeat "one." Breathe easily and naturally.

- Continue for 10 to 20 minutes.
- You may open your eyes to check the time, but do not use an alarm.
- When you finish, sit quietly for several minutes, at first with your eyes closed and later with your eyes open. Do not stand up for a few minutes.
- Do not worry about whether you were successful in attaining a deep level of relaxation.
- Maintain a passive attitude and permit relaxation to occur at its own pace.
- When distracting thoughts occur, try to ignore them by not dwelling upon them and return to repeating "one."
- With practice, the response should come with little effort.
- Practice the technique once or twice daily, but not within two hours after any meal, since the digestive processes seem to interfere with the elicitation of the Relaxation Response.

Later in his book "Beyond Relaxation Response", Dr. Benson advised clients to devise personalized but meaningful mantras in 1 or 2 words or a small motivational phrase. eg relax, peace, happy, all is well, etc to be repeated during exhalation instead of ''one".

TM is a prototype of meditation. It has been well studied in clinical situations. Here let us understand the importance of parasympathetic autonomous nervous system. I am sorry I will have to use some technical words but you can easily understand the concept.

Activating the Parasympathetic Nervous System (PSNS) to Decrease Anxiety

The parasympathetic nervous system is an anatomically defined division of the autonomic nervous system, being that part whose motor components run in cranial nerves III, VII, IX, and X, and in the sacral nerves. It exerts its effects on autonomically controlled organs of the head, thorax, abdomen, and pelvis but not of the limbs or skin.

Parasympathetic preganglionic neurons have their cell bodies in the central nervous system and make synapses in the ganglia close to or in the walls of the organs they supply. Acetylcholine and nitric oxide are the major neurotransmitters of parasympathetic postganglionic neurons.

The PSNS promotes a rest-and-digest response and performs the following functions: Dilates blood vessels leading to the GI tract, increasing blood flow; Constricts the bronchiolar diameter when the need for oxygen has diminished; Causes constriction of the pupil and contraction of the ciliary muscle to the lens allowing for closer vision; Stimulates salivary gland secretion and accelerates peristalsis; Stimulates sexual arousal.

Activation of the Sympathetic nervous system (SNS) mediates fight or flight response during activation of stress, while activation of the parasympathetic nervous system (PSNS) mediates rest & digest or feed & breed activities. It is a key to the relaxation response – body's antidote to stress response. Just as doing exercise stimulates SNS, doing certain activities must be stimulating PSNS. Some of them are deep breathing & conscious muscular relaxation.

When the parasympathetic nervous system is activated, it produces a calm and relaxed feeling in the mind and the body. People can learn to trigger their parasympathetic nervous system to immediately reduce their sense of anxiety and stress. This also lifts their mood, strengthens their immune system, and reduces their blood pressure.

Before Dr. Benson developed the Relaxation Response theme, Dr. Jacobson had developed progressive muscular relaxation, a way to purposefully tense & relax different groups of muscles, training the individual to recognize what it feels like to relax. It is one of the good methods to relieve tension. It is more of a physically oriented relaxation.

Dr. Edmund Jacobson invented this technique in the 1920s as a way to help his patients deal with anxiety. Dr. Jacobson felt that relaxing the muscles could relax the mind as well. The technique involves tightening one muscle group while keeping the rest of the body relaxed and then releasing the tension, on purpose & training the mind to feel the relaxation.

Progressive muscular relaxation (PMR) therapy is generally safe and doesn't require professional guidance. Sessions typically last no more than 20-30 minutes, making it manageable for people with busy schedules. You can practice the techniques at home using the instructions from a book, website, or tape. Joy Rains advises beginning the relaxation therapy with a breathing exercise and then moving from the feet up.

She suggests the following exercises: Progressive Muscular Relaxation

Bring your attention to your feet. Point your feet downward, and curl your toes under. Tighten your toe muscles gently, but don't strain. Notice the tension for a few moments, then release and notice the relaxation. Repeat. Become aware of the difference between the muscles when they're tensed and when they're relaxed.

Now dorsiflex the toes towards you, tighten the muscles, feel it & relax, feeling the relaxation attentively. Continue to tense and relax the leg muscles from the foot to the abdominal area. Feet, Calves, Thighs, Gluteals are muscle groups to be tightened & then allowed to relax.

Then gently tighten the muscles of your abdomen by trying to take abdominal muscles towards the spine, contracting inwards & upwards, but don't strain. Notice the tension for a few moments. Then release and notice the relaxation during exhalation. Repeat. Become aware of the difference between the tensed muscles and the relaxed muscles.

Then for shoulders and neck, very gently shrug your shoulders straight up towards your ears. Don't strain. Feel the tension for a few moments, release it, and then feel the relaxation. Repeat. Notice the difference between the tensed muscles and the relaxed muscles. Then try to squeeze both scapulae by bringing them towards the spine, tense, feel & relax.

Focus on the neck muscles, first tensing and then relaxing until you feel total relaxation in this area. Then focus on muscles of face, jaw & eyes. Lastly, clench your fists tightly & hold & release & feel the relaxation.

Localized technique: In general tighten a group of muscles for a count of 10 & then allow it to relax for a count of 20. You can also apply relaxation therapy to specific parts of the body.

Nicole Spruill is a speech specialist. She uses Jacobson's relaxation technique to help professionals who sing or do a lot of public speaking to prevent and recover from vocal cord strain. Here is the three-step process.

Spruill recommends: Close your hands tightly to feel the tension. Hold for 5 seconds, and slowly allow the fingers to release one by one until they're completely relaxed. Press your lips tightly together and hold for 5 seconds, feeling the tension. Slowly release. The lips should be completely relaxed and barely touching after the release. Finally, press your tongue against the roof of your mouth for 5 seconds, and notice the tension. Slowly relax the tongue until it's sitting on the floor of the mouth and your jaws are slightly unclenched. (By the way, lips have the maximum density of parasympathetic nerve endings).

Basically, tensing and relaxing activates stretch fibers, which are sensed by the cholinergic nerve endings, so also dilatation of small vessels increases the release of nitric oxide & vice versa.

Many teachers advocate 10 seconds contraction, 20 seconds relaxation, with 3 deep & slow abdominal breaths before moving to the next group of muscles. It works to reduce anxiety & work-related stress. During all these processes, concentrate your attention on feeling/perceptions generated in muscles. Don't get carried away by thoughts or memories or plans. Do the exercise in the "here & now".

What is Deep Breathing?

You can notice that during acute stress, your breathing becomes faster, shallower & chest bound. This is due to the overactivation of the sympathetic nervous system. It appears logical that on purpose, slow, deep abdominal breathing, with exhalation prolonged than inhalation by 20% -30% will activate the parasympathetic nervous system & offset acute effects of SNS overstimulation caused by stress response.

Have you ever noticed how we breathe when we get up first in the morning? Or at night when we are just entering the kingdom of sleep? We go to sleep only after our breathing is slow & abdominal. Or watch a baby, it is always breathing abdominally.

So when you on purpose slow your breathing, make it deep abdominal, your brain gets the signal that there is no danger, you are safe.

Indian seers had a great understanding of the effects of deep breathing on calming the mind, and they have offered **Pranayama**, a detailed system of using breaths for the health of the body and mind.

Imagine there is a balloon in your abdomen which gets inflated each time you inhale through the nose. Slowly inflate it & then deflate it slowly while you exhale through pursed lips. You can make a hissing sound while exhaling. Do this for 3 -5 minutes & feel your relaxation. Bring down your respiratory rate to 6 per minute.

Remember to concentrate fully on the sensation of air passing through the nose going into the abdomen, slowly distending it & then slowly being exhaled.

CHAPTER FOUR

Breathing Exercises for Relaxation

Deep breathing is one of the best ways to lower the effects of stress on the body. This is because when you breathe deeply, it sends a message to your brain to calm down and relax. The brain then sends this message to your body. Those things that happen when you are stressed, such as increased heart rate, fast breathing, and high blood pressure, all decrease as you breathe deeply to relax.

How do you do breathing exercises?

There are lots of breathing exercises you can do to help relax. The first exercise given below, belly breathing, is simple to learn and easy to do. It's best to start from here if you have never done breathing exercises before. The other exercises are more advanced. All of these exercises can help you relax and relieve stress.

Belly breathing (Diaphragmatic breathing)

Belly breathing is easy to do and very relaxing. Try this basic exercise anytime you need to relax or relieve stress.

- Sit or lie flat in a comfortable position.
- Put one hand on your belly just below your ribs and the other hand on your chest.
- Take a deep breath in through your nose, and let your belly push your hand out. Your chest should not move.

- Breathe out through pursed lips as if you were whistling. As you exhale slowly, feel the hand on your belly go in.
- Do this breathing exercise 3 to 10 times.
- Take your time with each breath.
- During breathing, keep all your attention on the sensations in your breathing apparatus. Do not think.
- Notice how you feel at the end of the exercise.

Next steps: After you have mastered belly breathing, you may want to try one of these more advanced breathing exercises.

Try all three, and see which one works best for you:

1) 4-7-8 breathing
2) Roll breathing
3) Morning breathing

4-7-8 breathing -

This exercise also uses belly breathing to help you relax. You can do this exercise either sitting or lying down.

- To start with put one hand on your belly and the other on your chest as in the belly breathing exercise.
- Take a deep, slow breath from your belly, and silently count from 1 to 4 as you breathe in.
- Hold your breath, and silently count from 1 to 7.
- Breathe out completely as you silently count from 1 to 8.
- Try to get all the air out of your lungs by the time you count to 8.
- Repeat 3 to 7 times or until you feel calm.
- Notice how you feel at the end of the exercise.

Roll breathing

Roll breathing helps you to develop full use of your lungs and to focus on the rhythm of your breathing. You can do it in any position. But while you are learning, it is best to lie on your back with your knees bent.

- Put your left hand on your belly and your right hand on your chest. Notice how your hands move as you breathe in and out.
- Practice filling your lower lungs by breathing so that your "belly" (left) hand goes up when you inhale and your "chest" (right) hand remains still. Always breathe in through your nose and breathe out through your mouth. Do this 8 to 10 times.
- When you have filled and emptied your lower lungs 8 to 10 times, add the second step to your breathing: inhale first into your lower lungs as before, and then continue inhaling into your upper chest.
- Breathe slowly and regularly. As you do so, your right hand will rise and your left hand will fall a little as your belly falls. As you exhale slowly through your mouth, make a quiet, whooshing sound as first your left hand, and then your right hand, falls. As you exhale, feel the tension leaving your body, as you become more and more relaxed.
- Practice breathing in and out in this way for 3 to 5 minutes. Notice that the movement of your belly and chest rises and falls like the motion of rolling waves. Notice how you feel at the end of the exercise.
- Practice roll breathing daily for several weeks until you can do it almost anywhere. You can use it as an instant relaxation tool anytime you need one.
- Caution: Some people get dizzy the first few times they try roll breathing. If you begin to breathe too fast or feel lightheaded, slow your breathing. Get up slowly.

Morning breathing

- Try this exercise when you first get up in the morning to relieve muscle stiffness and clear clogged breathing passages. Then use it throughout the day to relieve back tension.
- From a standing position, bend forward from the waist with your knees slightly bent, letting your arms dangle close to the floor.
- As you inhale slowly and deeply, return to a standing position by rolling up slowly, lifting your head last.
- Hold your breath for just a few seconds in this standing position.
- Exhale slowly as you return to the original position, bending forward from the waist.
- Notice how you feel at the end of the exercise.

Remember that in all these breathing techniques you should fully concentrate on sensations produced by the process & do not think anything.

Few more Breathing Exercises :

If you are comfortable with the previous exercises then you can move on to some more

1) Anulom Vilom Pranayam: Alternate nostril breathing (*Nadi Shodhanam*).

Close one nostril, take a deep breath through open nostril, now close the nostril through which you inhaled & then exhale through the opened nostril which you had closed. Do this for 15 breaths & then switch the nostrils & again take 15 deep breaths through opposite nostril & exhale through one which was closed before. All the time give full attention/concentration to sensations of air moving through nostrils.

2) Breathing clouds:

Sit comfortably, close your eyes, settle into the rhythm of deep breathing. Now imagine the fresh, pure, cool air which you are inhaling is purifying & detoxifying your whole body & mind. Visualize this air to be of golden white colour, from your nose it travels to your head, then it enters the spinal canal & through the nerves it passes to all organs & cells, purifying & detoxifying them. Now as you exhale, visualize that the air leaving your body is dirty air, say gray-black in colour, like a cloudy smoke symbolizing all stress, all worries, toxins leaving your body, brain & mind. After 5-10 min. you see the gray colour of air which you are breathing out is fading & it also is becoming off whitish golden, pure, symbolizing the release of stress & tension.

CHAPTER FIVE

Autogenic Training for Reducing Anxiety

Stress can arouse anger or fear when the body is preparing to either fight or run away. So that for the fight, muscles of jaw, fist, shoulder & neck get tightened & for flight, muscles of calf, thighs & back get tightened. Therefore, after the day's work, you will notice you are fatigued & these muscle groups have become tense.

Autogenic trainingis a type of relaxation technique that can be used to help reduce anxiety, including that experienced as a part of Social Anxiety Disorder (SAD). It can be incorporated into regular treatment such as cognitive-behavioral therapy (CBT) or used on your own as a self-help strategy.

Autogenic training is a relaxation technique first introduced by a German psychiatrist Johannes Heinrich Schultz in 1932. Schultz noticed that individuals undergoing hypnosis entered a relaxed state in which they experienced feelings of heaviness and warmth, and he sought to recreate that state in people to reduce tension and anxiety.

How do you do 'Autogenic training`?

First, find a quiet place that is free from distractions. Lie on the floor or recline in a chair. Loosen any tight clothing and remove glasses or contacts. Rest your hands in your lap or on the arms of the chair.

Like in Progressive Muscular Relaxation (PMR), here also, groups of muscles are attended to, giving suggestions to increase warmth, vascularity & heaviness. This is conductive of relaxed feeling.

To each muscle group, you mentally give suggestions like "My feet are relaxed, my feet are heavy, warm & numb". Say this 6 times & move to the next muscle group. As you progress to the next group take 3 deep breaths. Slowly & slowly all major muscles will be relaxed & you will feel calm, peaceful & relaxed. You can use similar step by step approach as suggested to in PMR.

Royal Road of stress dissipation - Meditation

All of us have an inner parent or inner boss. Sitting deep inside us, it is in a constant judgmental mode, constantly chattering, nagging, pestering & commenting. It is highly criticizing, never satisfied with itself & never allowing us to be at rest.

Moreover, our brain is constantly producing thoughts. Just as our lungs constantly breathe, our hearts constantly beat, similarly, our brains constantly think. This constant thinking activity consumes a lot of energy that leaves us exhausted. Normally, thinking is a reaction to what we perceive through our senses. Thoughts also spring up in response to memories, or by association with futuristic plans.

Actually, thoughts are separate from each other, following each other like bougies of a train. but they follow each other in such a fast succession that we never sense the gaps between two thoughts. But we can learn to slow the rate of the thinking process, observe our thoughts non-judgmentally, without getting involved, & try to catch 'the gap' between two consecutive thoughts. This space between two thoughts is our real restful break.

Once we get the taste of this relaxed non-demanding alertness, we feel the freedom in just being in this moment, in the `now` or in `the gap`. Hinduism & Buddhism have a long tradition of this discipline. This process of remaining alert and becoming aware of the still and clear `gap` in between two thoughts is called **Meditation.**

Meditation is staying focused in the present moment and allowing our inner voice to become silent. When we are in `the gap`, we are free of ghosts from the past, imagined enemies, future deadlines, worrisome ruminations, and anticipations. We reclaim our own space where we can stand free from time pressure, step back from the chaos of life situations & just be. Later, when we become an expert in withdrawing from our involvement and entanglements, we can then do some rational thinking, take stock of the situation & start proactive construction of life according to our values and priorities.

Meditation: Let us claim our Inner Space!

Awareness is the specialized part of consciousness. Awareness has two ends. Subject, that is you, & an object, that you focus your attention on to. When you pay attention to an external object or internal objects like your thoughts, feelings, etc you forget yourselves & are focused and lost in the object or carried away by your thoughts or feelings.

In other words, when you are paying attention to something, you forget yourself. When we remember our self as a subject, while still paying attention to an object; we can be said to be as aware of ourselves as being aware of that object.

Meditation is this - becoming aware of our being aware.

Meditation is when the subject is aware of himself while still maintaining the focus of attention on the object. Imagine a rubber band. When it is taut, it has tension; when we release it, it is back to its original self relaxed form, without tension & at rest. At this resting state, the rubber band has undone its tension.

Therefore as Rupert Spira says, *Meditation is not something we do but something we cease to do.*

So, actually, meditation is not a practice. Becoming something else other than what we are, needs practice, but just being what we actually are, is just being ourselves, staying in our natural state, by letting go of any effort to become something else. Then why so many instructions about preparation, posture, breathing, etc?

Compare it to the situation of a person who has lost the natural normal art of going to sleep effortlessly. He is given instructions about sleep hygiene. Something like 'don't drink caffeinated drinks after the evening', 'don`t watch TV/ MOBILE after certain time', 'make the room dark', 'remove distractions', etc - it helps. These instructions by themselves don't induce sleep, but they help to remove distractions and allow natural sleep reflex and rhythm to set in. It is not sleep itself, but conductive of sleep. Similarly, all instructions about meditation are conductive to a meditative state, which is our natural state by birth and which we have forgotten or lost in the chaos of complexities of living. Just as once you retrieve the art of sleeping you can sleep without any aid, naturally; similarly, once you recover the art of just being, without any distraction, then you don't need practice to create an atmosphere conducive to meditation. You can just 'be', anytime anywhere.

Health benefits of Meditation

Meditation has many health benefits and is a highly effective way to relieve stress and maintain a healthier lifestyle. With practice, meditation becomes both more of an easy habit to maintain and more of an effective one as well, given that it builds resilience to stress over time. Putting in the effort to learn and practice meditation can actually transform your experience of stress in your life.

Proven benefits of Meditation -

- Reduces Stress
- Reduces hypertension
- Controls anxiety
- Helps in deaddiction
- Promotes emotional health
- Reduces chronic inflammation
- Enhances self-awareness

- Increases memory & attention span
- Reduces aging
- Helps control pain
- Improves Sleep

Meditation is a gift of the East to the whole world. Meditation is like a bath for the mind. Our mind is like a blackboard on which each sensory input, each thought, each motion, each memory is scribbling something, ultimately leading to the blackboard being overloaded, crowded, messed up, cluttered, disorganized, and difficult to understand anything at all. This overload exhausts us, decreases our concentration, impairs our perceptions, slows our thinking.

Meditation is like an eraser or a duster that cleans the blackboard, refreshes us, and prepares us for the next day again. Our concentration improves, perceptions sharpen, interpretations mature & wisdom - insight arises.

Types of Meditation

Some types of meditations are exclusive or restrictive & others are inclusive or opening up in their style. Exclusive meditations focus on only one thought, or image, or sound, or mantra to the exclusion of all other thoughts, and stimuli.

Transcendental meditation (TM) is a prototype of exclusive meditation. They are techniques of concentration. While in inclusive meditation, nothing is to be excluded, the mind is allowed to wander freely, but awareness takes the position of a witness. Witnessing awareness stays in the `here & now` and just observes whatever is happening in this 'now'. It sees thoughts, images, memories as floating in the vast space of consciousness but does not get involved in it, does not invest emotionally into anything. For this to happen, the mind has to maintain awareness of becoming aware.

This is also called a detached observation or choiceless awareness. The goal is to observe the observer. Mindfulness is just a name for becoming mindful in the present moment. We can pay full attention and be mindful of our body parts, or we can pay attention to how the external physical world is trying to contact us. We can pay full attention to the sensations like sounds, touch, pressure, feel of air passing through our nasal passages or the tone & rhythm of a sound or a chant.

We can also develop aware mindfulness of thoughts passing like clouds moving through the inner space of our mind. In mindfulness meditations, we are strengthening two of our mental faculties. The first faculty is of mindfulness, which is paying full focused attention to chosen object by becoming aware of whatever is arising & the second faculty is maintaining a witnessing attitude of not judging, not clinging, not getting involved, allowing anything to appear or disappear from our focus by letting it go.

When we start to develop this faculty of mindfulness by giving full attention to an object, we often forget it in no time. Some thought pops up & we are carried away. We forget what we are doing and are lost in the jungle of thought. Somehow again we remember that we are trying to pay attention and we are back on our chosen object.

This happens so many times that the practitioner can get frustrated. But this is what our monkey mind is. In fact, this is the natural tendency of our mind, which we don't notice in day-to-day busy activities. It is this tendency of mind which you are going to bring under control when you persist in your practice. When the awareness of this loss of focus arises, again witnessing attitude also arises, & you resume your practice of mindfulness.

Both exclusive & inclusive meditations give strength to the faculty of awareness & facilitate the development of a calm & peaceful state of mind. However, this can take years of practice. Both types of meditations decrease the body's basal metabolic rate, heart rate, blood pressure. The meditative state is associated with decreased oxygen consumption, decreased muscle tension & an increase in the alpha waves in the brain. Science has proved that meditation is a real antidote to stress and improved mental health.

CHAPTER SIX

How to Begin a Basic Meditation Practice?

There are many different ways to meditate and this technique is one of the most basic. This is conductive to achieving a state of mindful awareness. With practice, you can use this technique to feel inner peace whenever you need it.

Here's how to begin a basic meditation practice:

Step 1: Get Into a Comfortable Position

Choose a quiet place & time where you will not be distracted easily. Think, plan & choose where and how you'll sit. Many people like to sit in a comfortable chair while others prefer to sit cross-legged on the ground. You want to be able to completely relax while still staying awake. Don't try any difficult or abnormal posture.

Posture should not give you more stress! You should sit with a straight back but the back should be supported. Don't do meditation in reclining or lying down position, these are more conductive of sleep rather than alert watchfulness. Ensure that your posture is correct. But don't strain. It is easier to stay awake through long meditations if your back is straight.

If you begin your meditation practice with this in mind, your body will become used to the position as you plan to sit for longer time. or those who are much stressed, it is advisable to do progressive muscular relaxation first & then start medication. If you choose to sit in a chair, sit towards the front of the seat and place your feet firmly on the floor. This will improve your posture and help you concentrate on your practice. Feel gratitude that you are getting a chance to do meditation.

Step 2: Close Your Eyes Gently & remind yourself of your intention.

When you are in a comfortable position, allow your eyes to slowly shut down. Do not squeeze your eyes tightly. Mentally remind yourself that you are just going to relax. You are going to remain as an alert witness of anything that comes up to claim your attention.

To anchor your wandering attention, you are going to keep your attention on whatever sounds are coming up to you or you will keep your attention on the movement of air while breathing. You want to relax all of your facial muscles. You may want to keep your eyes half-open. Do not focus on anything if you are doing 'eyes open' meditation. Instead of focusing, learn to defocus, don't move eyes but be aware of all of your field of vision.

Try to focus on what is in your surroundings, without actually looking there. At this stage, your goal is to relax every part of your body. If you feel some tension in certain parts of your body, take a deep breath and allow it to relax that part of the body. When smile muscles are activated, your brain gets a signal that there is no danger. It is relaxing. So smile up a bit if you feel ok with it.

Step 3: Now start paying attention to the breathing

The air which goes in & which comes out as you breathe in & out. You can pay attention to how this air feels, warm or cold. Listen to the faint sound the breath makes and be aware of the gap between Inspiration & Expiration. Let the breathing be natural If you find it difficult to concentrate at the tip of the nose, you may find it easier to anchor on the sensation of your tummy as it goes up & down with each in & out breath.

Step 4: Try to keep your awareness of yourself as a watcher of breaths or upcoming thoughts.

This is the part of meditation that takes the most practice and it can cause the most frustration. Distractions in the form of random thoughts will keep arising, you may get trapped in a chain of thoughts without you being aware of it. But as soon as you notice it, smile, let go of these thoughts and come back to your anchor. Learning to do this during your meditation practice is actually the practice of letting go.

This can help you to be able to let redundant things go from the rest of your life as well (nonclinging attitude). As you start to pay attention to breathing, thoughts will arise & you will lose yourself again and again.

The idea is to stay unattached to thoughts of any kind. That means that, if the inner voice of your chattering mind speaks up, gently "shush" it and bring your awareness back to the breath. Opt for internal silence & ignore your thoughts. You can refocus on the sensation of breathing & bringing your awareness to ingoing & outgoing breath.

Tip: Do not be discouraged if you cannot clear your thoughts completely. Our minds are constantly filled with thoughts and even the most experienced meditators find it difficult to remain silent. The goal is to recognize the thought, then mentally ask it to go away; don't indulge into it, let it go & you can come back to attend to the breath. Again and again, such distractions will increase your power of paying attention.

Step 5: Keep Going - Keep awareness that you are witnessing consciousness anchored to your breathing & that's all.

That's it, really! Keep letting go of any thoughts that may pop into your mind. The longer you practice, the quiet spaces in between two thoughts will become longer and more frequent. You're already on the road to the great gift you can offer yourself, your witnessing attitude - meditation.

After 20 minutes, come back to normal awareness, take a few deep breaths & feel the gratitude that you could complete the meditation session.

A Few Tips to Help You improve your Meditation Practice.

Give it time. Success in Meditation takes practice, practice & persistent practice.

Realize that there is no perfect meditation session. Sometimes you will enter the witness mode quickly, feel relaxed and peaceful, while at other times you will have difficulty in maintaining the calm, you will get easily carried away by your thoughts, and both these scenarios are ok. They both are witnessing mindfulness sessions of meditation.

Don't create more stress by having some high expectations. There is no 'perfect' meditation session or rather, I would say, every meditation session is perfect by itself. The more you get distracted in a session, the more you have experienced your monkey mind. The fact that you recognized that you got carried away and could disentangle from the web of thoughts to come back to awareness is the success in itself. Cheer up, pat on your back and restart the witnessing process. After all, you are developing a new habit, it will take time.

Start with small sessions and work up to longer sessions. Begin with a short session of 5 minutes. After you are comfortable, move to 10 or 15 minutes and proceed this way until you are comfortable meditating for 20 – 30 minute sessions.

With practice, this type of meditation becomes easier and more effective. You will come out of a meditation session feeling relaxed and refreshed, ready to face the rest of your day. You should remain aware that you are witnessing consciousness, observing your thoughts as if they are clouds or birds in the sky. It is ok for birds to fly overhead but don't allow them to make a nest in your head.

Meditation can not go 'wrong'. Whatever you do, it is always 'right', whether you feel peaceful or not. Don't expect anything, accept life as it comes. This is a training in acceptance, non-striving (not attempting to change anything), letting go & remaining as a witness.

When you get up from your session, carry the idea of being a witness to all this drama of life. Before you act, talk or plan some project, go to your private space of `the gap`, sense your freedom to be, and then take the decision to act, talk or plan in proactive way. You are not a robot to behave impulsively or reactively.

This is how meditation will affect your life. You will be more peaceful, you will not cling to things, thoughts, emotions, relations etc. When time comes you will let these things go by naturally. You will be more content, joyful. You will engage with life but not get involved. You will love all creation without attachment. It is like allowing dirty muddy lake water to settle down by itself. If you do anything it is going to be muddy again.

So just patiently allow the calm to happen. Inside our head, there is a chatter-box, a voice in our head. It never stops, and keeps on talking continuously. Interestingly, as soon as you become aware of it & start listening to it, by paying attention on purpose - a non-judgemental attention, it stops!!! Albeit temporarily.

Because the mind runs on your resistance. The more you resist, the wilder it becomes. So just observe. Usually, many beginners feel it is difficult to stop this chatterbox, which is constantly on. It appears as if it will never stop.

The mind wanders. But the important thing is not to judge oneself (categorize as good or bad meditator), simply stay in awareness. The mind never stops, even for experienced meditators. Focused attention is the initial step. It leads to insight and compassion.

Wisdom is the ultimate aim. The first wisdom that will dawn upon you is that none of the states you perceive is constant, it is always changing. Sometimes you may find it most difficult to meditate when you are in emotional pain. Sitting quietly with the mind at that moment seems to be more challenging than distracting it.

Studies also suggest that many people experience worsening of their emotional state when they begin meditating. It is hard to acknowledge the pain and not judge yourself or others while sitting alone with your mind. But keep practicing; it is like preparing the mind for the next impact because now it knows that this too will pass away, it is already changing, so that the next reaction is more measured and controlled.

Meditation is to increase your observing and witnessing capacity, a step back so that you won't react impulsively. To help us develop our awareness, we must practice. So keep meditating. Our body is always in "here & now", it is our mind that wanders, so we use body sensations, as the anchor. e.g breathing & awareness of body - body scan. You can also use a Mantra, Om, or the Name of God as an anchor just like breathing.

The witnessing awareness should be on guard to see how thoughts are trying to intrude in & dismiss/neglect them. If prayer is talking to God, then meditation is listening to God. Imagine you have dialed a phone to God. He has picked it up & he will talk at any moment. It may be a whisper or just a word or so. Be intense and attentive, your life depends on it. So with intense awareness - Listen, Listen, & Listen. The listening mode is meditation.

When we are seeing a movie, the picture, the colour, the sounds keep on constantly changing. Our attention is hijacked by these changing realities. We can not become aware of the movie screen as long as we are involved in, engrossed in, and affected by the drama of the movie. Once we start becoming aware of the screen, the movie does not stop, but loses its grip. The movie still goes on but we are not affected by it, by the drama. When we meditate, we become aware of our consciousness, like becoming aware of the movie screen while still watching the movie. Everything is happening on the screen of our awareness. Awareness is always there. The screen has to be there for the movie to be seen.

Awareness has to be there for the world to be perceived but we are not aware of it. Being aware of our background awareness is meditation.

Awareness is meditative when it is aware of itself. When we come to the present moment on purpose, we become aware of all physical things happening now, we actually become aware of our capacity to be aware of all these things which are always happening even if we are aware or not. When we start paying attention, the factor which has been added is our awareness. Being aware of becoming aware is meditation.

Awareness has to be there for the world to be perceived but we are not aware of it. Being aware of our background awareness is meditation. Awareness is meditative when it is aware of itself. When we come to the present moment on purpose, we become aware of all physical things happening now, we actually become aware of our capacity to be aware of all these things which are always happening even if we are aware or not.

When we start paying attention, the factor which has been added is our awareness. Being aware of becoming aware is meditation.

CHAPTER SEVEN

Mindfulness

Mindfulness - This word has nearly become synonymous with meditation.

If you've heard of or read about mindfulness meditation - you may be wondering what it exactly is.

What is mindfulness?

Mindfulness is a type of meditation in which you focus on being intensely aware of what you're sensing and feeling in the moment, without interpretation or judgment. Practicing mindfulness involves breathing methods, body scan and other practices to relax the body and mind and help reduce stress.

Most of the time, we are never in our body nor are we aware of our surroundings. Our mind is anywhere but here & in anytime but in the now. Spending too much time planning, problem-solving, daydreaming, or thinking negative or random thoughts can be draining. It can also make you more likely to experience stress, anxiety, and symptoms of depression.

Practicing mindfulness exercises can help you direct your attention away from this kind of thinking and engage with the actual world around you. It is suggested that you start by bringing mindful awareness to some otherwise routine activity such as washing the dishes or eating a meal, brushing teeth, or putting on shoes, drinking tea, or going for a walk.

Slow down & pay attention. decide and on purpose give your attention to touch, smell, sounds around you. Don't name them, don't try to identify their source. Just be like a small child seeing the world with eyes full of curiosity.

What are the benefits of Mindfulness?

Mindfulness has been studied in many clinical trials. The overall evidence supports the effectiveness of this type of meditation for various conditions, including Stress, Anxiety, Chronic Pain, Depression, Insomnia, and High blood pressure (hypertension). Preliminary research indicates that mindfulness meditation can also help people with asthma, fibromyalgia & migraine.

Mindfulness Meditation can help you experience thoughts and emotions with greater balance and acceptance. Mindfulness meditation has also been shown to improve attention, decrease job burnout, improve sleep, improve diabetes control & decrease accidents.

What are some examples of mindfulness exercises?

There are many simple ways to practice mindfulness. Some examples include: Pay attention. It's hard to slow down and notice things in a busy world. Try to take the time to experience your environment with all of your senses — touch, sound, sight, smell, and taste. For example, when you eat a favorite food, take the time to smell, taste, and truly enjoy it, eat very slowly, savour it, close your eyes to relish it. Live in the moment. Try to intentionally bring an open, accepting, and discerning attention to everything you do.

Find joy in simple pleasures. Accept yourself. Treat yourself the way you would treat a good friend. Focus on your breathing. When you have negative thoughts, try to sit down, take few deep breaths and close your eyes. Focus on your breath as it moves in and out of your body. Sitting and breathing for even for just a minute or two can help. You can also try more structured mindfulness exercises, such as scanning your whole body.

Body scan meditation.

Lie on your back with your legs extended and arms at your sides, palms facing up. Focus your attention slowly and deliberately on each part of your body, in order, from toe to head or head to toe. Be aware of any sensations, emotions, or thoughts associated with each part of your body, as if you are exploring your body from the inside. If you find any part painful, stressed then do a short session of progressive muscular relaxation & then try body scan again. Body scanning is a great way of coming in contact with your own body.

You will find a sense of relaxation; warmth & heaviness slowly spreads over your body. All the time your mind will try to highjack your attention by generating thoughts, memories etc but just neglect it and come back to paying attention as to how your body feels.

Incorporating different types of meditations

- **Sitting meditation**- Sit comfortably in a chair with your back straight, feet flat on the floor, and hands in your lap. Breathing through your nose, focus on your breath moving in and out of your body. If physical sensations or thoughts interrupt your meditation, note the experience and then return your focus to your breath. In the beginning, to help you focus on your anchor you can start counting each breath when you exhale. Like inhale 1, inhale 2, after count 6, restart from count 1.
- **Walking meditation**-. Find a quiet place 10 to 20 feet in length, and begin to walk slowly. Focus on the experience of walking, being aware of the sensations of standing, and the subtle movements that keep your balance. When you reach the end of your path, turn and continue walking, maintaining awareness of your sensations. To help you maintain awareness you can count steps in sync with breathing e.g. Inhale 2-3-4 Exhale 2-3-4. Adjust your own pace. You can walk still more slowly & mentally say to yourself: 'lifting, moving, landing & shifting', when you focus attention on lifting a foot, moving forward, landing on the ground & then shifting to other foot, respectively.

When and how often should you practice mindfulness exercises?

It depends on what kind of mindfulness exercise you plan to do. Simple mindfulness exercises can be practiced anywhere and anytime. Research indicates that engaging your senses outdoors in nature is especially beneficial, to relieve stress.

For more structured mindfulness exercises, such as body scan meditation or sitting meditation, you'll need to set aside time when you can be in a quiet place without distractions or interruptions.

You might choose to practice this type of exercise early in the morning before you begin your daily routine. Aim to practice mindfulness every day for about three months. Over time, you might find that mindfulness becomes effortless. Think of it as a commitment to reconnecting with and nurturing yourself.

You can remember SS BOG ie STOP, SMILE, BREATH (deep breath), OBSERVE (be mindful of everything for a minute) & Go. This can be done any number of times in a day. When we are rushing through the day, we are focussed on something we plan, or on the results of our actions, or some unfinished job in any of the areas of our life.

We eat but don't know what we ate, we travel but don't remember anything of the journey, we talk but don't remember what we talked about. Because we are mindless about it while we are doing it. We do not pay attention. We are on automatic pilot or default mode. Through our inattention, we create suffering, clinging & frustrations.

Stress is a measure of our inattention. We are absent in our life. Mindfulness means to be present here & now, at this moment, without expecting anything but with the spirit of a wonderful child with innocent eyes, ready to know, to see, touch, smell & meet this life which is constantly changing like a flowing river.

Mindfulness or meditation is not the only way to stress management. Multiple techniques are available. For a long-term solution to avoid the harmful effects of stress, one has to have a set of such techniques ready in their arsenal. What suits whom, at a given moment, differs from person to person. And one should know what suits them and apply the most effective solution in a given situation. Reading, listening to calming music, talking to friends, going for a walk are also some of the techniques to reduce stress.

When one finds it difficult to meditate in scheduled time due to emotional reasons or due to preoccupation with some thoughts, walking for some time before meditation, hot/ cold water bath before meditation, yogasana, exercise, and pranayam before meditation, or any combination of the above helps.

There are many Mindfulness exercises and many meditation techniques. When the mind is disturbed, those meditation techniques focusing outside the body help instead of those involving internal focus. You can also vary the intensity of the focus. When the focus is less intense, one can complete the meditation with more ease. Keeping schedule or consistency helps in the long run. Inattention to some of the sensory inputs or being on autopilot does not by itself cause suffering, clinging, and frustrations.

It's the way we react to thoughts, emotions, and images produced by gathering information mindlessly, inattentively that creates these negative states. Being continuously on full mindfulness mode to its full extent slows down our working and reduces efficiency. Autopilot has its own role and usefulness.

Mindfulness procedures modified (interspersed in between or mixed with autopilot mode) for the purpose of a given situation give us better results. Rather attending to these aspects will give us a good feeling and free us from the suffering which is associated with inattention.

So in short, planning, remembering, thinking, labelling, judging, are all parts of our activity, they have their rightful place. Fine, but we have lost balance. Mindfulness is not given its due place. Just as we need a balance between the sympathetic and parasympathetic nervous systems, similarly automatic pilot, as well as mindfulness, both are required in balance, not one at the cost of the other. In fact, we have progressed due to our ability to be on autopilot, but our relaxation, happiness, sense of belonging are in the field of mindfulness.

You have to use both judiciously. We have to learn to slow down, we have to avoid multitasking, etc. A simple resolve like, ' I will be mindful of all what I am doing for the next 2 min' can help you in getting a taste of it every 1 or 2 hourly. Setting aside 10 min can be overwhelming in the beginning, but soon it can become a tempting inactivity.

At the beginning of sitting mindfulness, the practice of awareness of breath can be helped by breath counting. You can also give a try to reverse counting. Meditation is for awakening; relaxation is its side effect. You awaken to your witnessing mode, step back & observe mode, come in contact with life which is happening now and here & avoid the tendency to get lost in the past or future.

Mindfulness is synonymous with meditation. In fact, our minds are so full of so many thoughts that we are lost in them. We forget ourselves. When we bring our attention to the present tense, here & now, for the first time we start waking up. The grip of thoughts, plans, agendas, memories, deadlines and so many emotions attached to them, all become loose.

We take up an anchor, sensations of breathing or body scan, later on even thought & emotion as an anchor for maintaining awareness and incorporated it in mindfulness meditation practice. To escape from stress or the boredom of the routine hum-drum of life people often go to watch a movie, read a book, listen to their favorite music. They kill time, they forget about their problems. But once this activity is over they are back to the stressful & boring, mediocre life. Is this meditation? No, it is engrossment, not meditation. In these activities you forget basically yourself.

When you forget yourself you forget your problems also. In mindfulness & in any type of meditation you are encouraged to become more conscious of yourself, more aware of your body, your surroundings. This causes you to feel more alive. You learn to become witness of your life, your thoughts, your drama, your role. You bring your awareness totally to an act but you don't forget yourself; you maintain awareness of the whole process. This doesn't change your problems, your stress but it changes you. You become more attentive, more slow, more deliberate, more proactive. Your impulsiveness decreases. You become less reactive but more sensitive. You become more peaceful. You start regaining control. Your ability to take joy from ordinary things increases. You become more loving but less attached. You allow things to be & learn to let go.

Buddha said, "while breathing, know that you are breathing - whether you are breathing a long breath or a short breath". You don't have to say this to yourself but just know it & remember that you are aware of it. *You should be present as a witness, which you are. This is not an imagination. All things are happening in your consciousness. Observing your consciousness as an independent observer is meditation.*

Time and again thoughts will intrude & you will lose yourself. Doesn't matter, it takes a very long time to be able to fully be aware of everything. But these glimpses will give rise to wisdom, so-called insight meditation. This is something you have to generate yourself. In Sitting meditation, you are being trained, to be aloof witness, to give your attention without involvement, to accept & to let go. This training you have to carry on the battlefield of the world. Spiritual meditations also elaborate upon loving, kindness, compassion, etc. This has been elaborated and embraced by Dr. Jon Kobat Zinn, pioneer of Mindfulness Based Stress Reduction (MBSR) program.

Spiritual Aspects of Meditation

There is a great tradition of meditation on the path of self-realization. **Karm-Yog**(doing your duty without any expectation of results), **Bhakti-Yog** (surrendering personal ego & agenda completely to the ultimate reality, seeing ultimate reality in everything, person & event, and therefore loving the whole creation), **Dnyan-Yog** (accepting the ever-existent unity of all living & nonliving creation- Adwaitism- & therefore remaining in the undivided universal consciousness as our & whole creations' reality (Sat-Chit-Anand) and **Dhyan-Yog** are accepted paths of God /Self Realization.

Dhyan-Yog has been greatly expounded in the Bhagvad-Gita & Dnyaneshwari. In spiritual meditation, one is advised self-inquiry (who I am?), bringing into awareness one's experience of being alive, `I AM` IS TO BE EXPERIENCED, not as this or that but as just pure, attribute less aliveness. Then this is to be maintained throughout waking consciousness as the witnessing principle. Depending upon the intensity of aspirant this witnessing principle then infiltrates all the stages of consciousness & all sheaths of the body. There are many realized masters in Hindu & Buddhist tradition & reader is advised to refer to their teachings.

Stress prone personalities & Resilience

Who is more prone to stress-induced damage? In the late 1960s, it was noticed that ischemic heart disease (IHD) was achieving epidemic proportions in developed countries. Many epidemiological studies were conducted to find out the risk factors for this epidemic. In 1964 Friedman & Roseman stumbled upon a personality type; which they named Type A personality, which was found to increase the risk of I.H.D. significantly. The behavioural pattern of Type A people is described as hurry, worry & curry. They are very impatient (Time urgency), often multitasking, very egoistic, super competitive and manipulative.

The most important character that emerged was hostile aggressiveness. Therefore, anger resolving strategies form the major coping skill for Type A personalities. When you cannot express anger, it turns inwards. Then it is identified as a different type of personality called personality D. Persons with personality D are also prone to IHD. They exhibit characteristics like worry, irritability, gloom, social inhibition & depression.

Dr. Dean Ornish, in his landmark book, states that love expressed through compassion is the missing component in patients with heart disease. Other personality types such as Codependent, hopeless-helpless personalities are also prone to stress-induced damage.

Coping Strategies:

Individuals differ in their resistance to stress. You must be aware that some people are resistant to stress while some are very prone. One answer lies in the dimension of optimism - pessimism. The optimistic people have a better mood, a higher number of natural killer cells & a higher number of helper T cells.

Optimists are problem-oriented. They understand the problem, focus on solving it, make specific plans to solve it & implement it. They are so focused that they refrain from other activities until the problem is solved. They make contact with others, seek their advice, and find a solution. Pessimistic people have a different coping strategy. Initially, they either deny that the problem exists or they avoid doing activities that generate stress and shy away from taking opinions & advice from others.

Resilience:

Many people display the ability to bounce back from personal setbacks. Resiliency is the ability to overcome the tremendous stress of trauma, loss & tragedy. Nietzsche has said, "That which doesn't kill us, makes us stronger".

The characteristics of Resilient people include optimism, courage, flexibility, humor, compassion & faith in a higher power. (Faith factor).

Resilience can come as a natural trait but can also be taught/ learned. It consists of -

1) Creating a positive attitude about life.

2) Focusing on problem-solving activities.

3) Being grateful for your assets.

4) Developing a supportive social engagement system.

5) Selfcare activities, developing a healthy lifestyle, exercise, proper nutrition, sleep, and meditation.

6) Humor - the ability to laugh at oneself without sacrificing self-esteem.

7) Having faith in higher life purpose, higher creative principle.

8) Practicing mindfulness, living life consciously.

9) Practicing self-responsibility & self-acceptance through self-love.

10) Practicing self-assertiveness.

Yoga to relieve stress

Yoga means to unite. It is the unification of body (I), mind (II) & soul (III) that is hinted at. Unification of all three dimensions of our existence, with our source energy, is no doubt healing. Done regularly, it has been shown to reduce the effects of stress on both, body & mind. In terms of exercise & stress relief, yoga means Hathayoga ('H' means Sun & 'tha' means moon, indicating balance).

Yogasanas have been studied in Hypertension, Cancer, Diabetes, Depression & Menopausal Syndrome. Yoga is a great relaxation technique & has been shown to positively change the expression of the genes related to the body's immune function. Yoga has been proved to be extremely helpful in PTSD (Post Traumatic Stress Disorder).

Yoga not only increases muscle strength, and flexibility but also improves balance. It also incorporates various breathing exercises & done properly under expert guidance, qualifies as a system of moving meditation. It includes Pranayama (the art of breathing), Asanas (postures, stretching,) Dharana, Dhyan & Samadhi (Various stages of Meditation).

It also expects moral & ethical qualities from aspirants. This whole science is expounded by Maharshi Patanjali in Yog Sutras.

Sun Salutations (Suryanamaskar):

This is a set of 12 yoga postures, which is a very good exercise for all major joints and muscles of the body & stretching exercise for the spine. It should be performed slowly with mindful attention to breathing, stretching & other sensations in the body.

Yogasanas specifically used to relieve stress:

- Tadasana
- Gomukhasana
- Aradha Chackrasana
- Trikonasan
- Bandh Konasan
- Pawan Muktasan
- Bhujangasan
- Paschittottanasan
- Ardha Matsyendrasan
- Matsyasan
- Dhanurasan
- Shavasana

Yogasana should be done early in the morning on an empty stomach. Slow, deliberate mindful attention to body sensations; Breathing slow and deep; Posture held for 40-45 seconds; Pauses in between; Shavasana at the end.

Music Therapy

Music is the language of the soul. Music has transcendental qualities & when you tune in to it, you get the experience of a higher power - divinity. Music goes beyond all languages or rather Music is a universal language.

Indian classical music is a very highly evolved art & its performance transports the performers & listeners both into a different world. Different Ragas evoke different moods & emotions. Many trials have proved the healing effects of music. Don Campbell suggests singing itself is therapeutic. Chanting is also a form of music; soft clean vowel sounds, soft in nature, which trail off into a slight hum. Musical notes or 'sur's are connected with different chakras, associated with different colours & different meditative thoughts or affirmations.

If you like music, you must experiment with different symphonies, ragas, find out which one soothes you & listen mindfully, for 15-20 minutes, avoiding all other distractions or thoughts. Raga Darbari, Todi, Malkauns, Des, Puriya, Bageshri, Marwa, Bhairavi are some of the soothing ragas which help to reduce hypertension & induce relaxation.

Don't select upbeat fast music which will be a boost to your adrenaline. Select calm, relaxing, slow music. You can also try nature sounds, Ocean sounds, streams or waterfall & the like. But listen intently with all your attention & get soaked in music.

Visualization

Mental imagery, colour therapy & light therapy are used in the process of visualization. Visualization is a technique used for thousands of years as a part of meditation. Active imagination used by sports persons or performers or before interviews has been credited to improve performance scores.

Our body & brain can not tell the difference between actual or imagined imagery & hence we get all the benefits from imagined scenarios. You can produce a peaceful natural image to aid in relaxation, you can see behavioural changes or performance changes with your own image (used in de-addiction & sports coaching programs) and you can also use imaginary trips inside your body.

For example, you can visualize the damaged tissues being healed/replaced (mostly used by cancer patients). Youtube sources can provide a plethora of tapes to visualize as an aid to meditation. Let us take an example & explore a visualization technique. Suppose you have difficulties in getting the knack of meditation. You know the theory but somehow are not able to practice it.

So go to a quiet place. Sit in a comfortable posture; close your eyes. Now on the screen of your mind (make as large a screen as you can) create a very relaxing, peaceful, natural scene. Put in all colours, sounds images that you want. Create a meditation seat.

Now you enter into the scene. Calmly, happily, playfully, slowly go to the seat & sit on it. Close your eyes & start meditation. See yourself successfully meditating, slow your breathing, now match your actual breathing with the breathing of you in the movie; synchronize with it. Yes, you got it!!

Laughter Therapy

(Comic Relief / Hasya Yoga)

In 1964, Norman Cousins, suffered from Ankylosing spondylitis, a debilitating illness affecting the spine & joints, causing severe pain & limitations of joint movements. His doctors had no medicine to offer. Norman was not a doctor but he read about his disease & decided to treat himself. He started seeing humourous, funny movies & cartoon shows, candid Camera & he ultimately completely recovered himself. He has written a book "Anatomy of illness" describing his recovery. There are many such stories. Humour therapy, was known to ancient physicians but was not thoroughly investigated until recently.

Dr. Madan Kataria, the founder of Hasya Yoga, has revolutionized comic relief therapy by arguing that the Body does not understand the difference between Humorous versus non-humorous laughter and so derives all the benefits of laughter.

Dr. William Fry has devoted his life to investigating humour therapy & now Humor therapy has acquired a status in Relaxation Therapies for stress reduction. Latest studies have demonstrated a decrease in salivary lgA Levels, a marker of the stress response, after laughter therapy. Crying, yawning, orgasm & laughter are the body's four ways of catharsis, out of which laughter can be employed by anybody.

Dr. Katariyas Hasya Yoga is a mixture of different types of laughter & breathing exercises with some dance. About 20 members gather in a garden or an open-air space & start laughing while maintaining an eye to eye contact. Soon the group starts giggling & laughing, no need to fake anymore. A meta-analysis of laughter-inducing therapies (social science & medicine 232 (2019) 473-48) has shown that simulated (non-humorous) laughter is more effective than spontaneous one, and laughter-inducing therapies can improve depression.

Meanwhile make your own library of comic books, candid camera, Tom & Jerry, PL Deshpande & Woodhouse. Start with your family members, friends & start your own laughter therapy. Start your own Hasya yoga club of simulated non-humorous laughter today itself.

CHAPTER EIGHT

POLYVAGAL theory - Importance of VAGUS NERVE

We have already stressed that nervous system is very fast to respond to the challenge posed by a stressful situation. Part of our nervous system that responds first & fast is our primitive nervous system – Autonomic Nervous System. It has two parts, Sympathetic Nervous System (SNS) and Para Sympathetic Nervous System (PSNS). THE VAGUS NERVE is the main nerve of parasympathetic system.

We have seen that activating the parasympathetic nervous system, opposes stress response mediated by the Sympathetic Nervous System. Activating the vagal nerve is the body's balancing strategy to decrease the effects of stress produced on the body by activation of the sympathetic system.

Now, excuse me for a little technical discussion. There are two Vagal nuclei, a dorsal one and a ventral one. Dorsal and vagal are technical terms to refer to the backside and front side in reference to a central point of the structure wherein these nuclei are situated.

Now there is a muscular partition between our chest and abdomen. This partitioning muscle is called the Diaphgram. The dorsal vagal nucleus caters to the organs below the diaphragm & ventral nucleus for the organs above the diaphgram muscle.

Now we commonly use two terms while studying animal behavior. One is phylogeny and the other is ontogeny.

Phylogeny means the study of the behavior belonging to the species as a whole, while ontogeny is the study pertaining to a single given animal out of that species. For example, study of primates such as monkeys and humans, as they belong to a species, is phylogenetic study; while study of only human behavior is ontogeny. Phylogenetic behavioural expressions are governed by vagal nuclei through the Vagal nerve & its branches. The multiple branches of the Vagus nerve are together called polyvagal nerve complex. This is therefore called polyvagal contribution to stress Response.

This was proposed by Dr. Stephen Porges. The Vagus nerve serves the parasympathetic nervous system, which is the calming aspect of our nervous system mechanics. The sympathetic system arouses & activates us. The parasympathetic system calms us down.

The polyvagal nervous system is a social engagement system; so it's a mixture of activation & calming. This helps us to navigate relationships. The ventral vagal system supports social engagement system, while the dorsal vagal system supports immobilization behaviours, both rest & digest or feed & breed. Sometimes, if the animal is in very much danger, has no time to take to flight or has no power to engage in fight, it gets immobilized (paralysed), or it can even feign death. Once it escapes danger, it can utilize its social engagement system to get help.

There are many interesting actions mediated through the Vagus nerve. The ventral vagal nerve supplies the middle ear, which filters out background noises to make it easier to hear the human voice. It also affects the facial muscles & the ability to make communicative facial expressions. Finally, it affects the larynx, vocal tone & vocal patterning helping us to create soothing sounds. The dorsal vagal nerve affects the infra-diaphragmatic organs (organs situated below the diaphragm). When it gets activated, it produces an immobilizing / faint or freeze response by immediately shutting down the effects of the sympathetic activation.

The Polyvagal Theory provided us with a more sophisticated understanding of the biology of safety and danger. It provides us with an understanding of a system, based on the subtle interplay between the visceral experiences of our own bodies and the voices and faces of the people around us. Speaking from point of social psychology and its role in stressful situations, it helps us to understand why a kind face or a soothing tone of voice can dramatically alter the way we feel.

It clarifies why knowing that we are seen and heard by the important people in our lives can make us feel calm and safe and why being ignored or dismissed can precipitate rage reactions or mental collapse. It helps us understand why attuning with another person can shift us out of disorganized and fearful states.

In short, Porges's theory makes us look beyond the effects of fight or flight and puts social relationships front and center in our understanding of stress. It also suggested new approaches to healing that focus on strengthening the body's system for regulating arousal and minimizing the impact of stress.

We are social animals!

The social stress reliever system comprises of certain people & pets who love you unconditionally. They can be your sympathetic friends, your Guru or God or the Higher power in which you trust & faithfully surrender to, your prayers, your gratitude, wherever you feel safe because of physical, emotional or even imagined or perceived support. All these constitute defenses against stressors. We are social animals.

We have seen that there are many ways of reducing impact of stress on our body and mind. Apart from progressive muscle relaxation, deep slow abdominal breathing, mindfulness meditations, seeking a loving, trusting, safe environment and many mind-body procedures (like Yoga, Massage, Qui – Gong etc) can reduce the impact of stress.

Viktor Frankl, one of the greatest psychiatrists of the twentieth century, survived the death camps of Nazi Germany. His little book, "Man's Search for Meaning", is one of those life-changing books that everyone should read. A world in which there was someone ready to listen to another's pain seems to the sufferer a world in which it was worthwhile to live.

On the other hand, the small act of listening attentively with love is the greatest gift we can give. Listening wholeheartedly, carefully is not only an act of mindfulness but it also activates polyvagal communication in the listener. When we listen with full concentration to a human voice, something happens through our ventral Vagus nucleus.

When we sense a danger in our surroundings, our body system is triggered to pick up more & more signals about it. One of such response is that our middle ear muscle, supplied by the Vagus nerve, adjusts the tone of middle ear muscles in such a way that we become more receptive to peripheral sounds, sounds of nature, of animals, of wind etc. We defocus our attention from human voice frequencies which are of much lower frequencies, than that produced by natural happenings.

So when we on purpose give our focused attention to somebody talking, our middle ear muscles change the settings to pick up low frequencies of human voice. This sends signals to brain that the environment is now not so dangerous, we can afford to listen to human voices; and alarm signals threshold can be raised. This itself gives a feeling of relief. Thus both the speaker and the listener benefit. This is how social interactions reduce our stress level.

What is positive psychology?

We are all slaves of our chemistry. With a little drop in sugar or salt, you cannot function normally. You have to correct it, to come back to original normal (homeostasis) status, before you can even think normally. Like sugar & salt, there are so many chemicals in our body which are always in flux. A huge effort is put by body to maintain them in `normal` state so that our body functions normally.

Our brain cells, `neurons`, connect with each other and talk to each other through specialized chemicals called Neurochemicals.

These neurochemicals are secreted by neurons where there are contact points (synapses), between two or more neurons. Neurochemicals like Dopamine, Serotonin, Oxytocin, and Endorphins carry different messages & mean different information.

The neurochemicals balance each other's actions to maintain normal neuronal functioning. Imbalance due to excess or deficit of a particular neurochemical can be associated with certain neuropsychiatric abnormalities. But it is a matter of oversimplification to say that Serotonin deficiency is the cause of depression, as it is the sum total of all neuro-bio-chemicals that can produce a variety of affective imbalances.

This imbalance is produced by poor adaptation to chronic stress. The imbalance may be casually related to chronic effects of stress e.g, anxiety states, depression, thinking disorders etc. Imbalance may also be related to aging, immune dysfunctions, activation of certain oncogenes. Magnetic resonance spectroscopy (MRS) holds promise for understanding neurochemical mechanisms associated with many neuropsychiatric disorders. Your longevity is dependent upon many factors one of which is balance of your neurochemicals. You can affect your neurochemical balance by your genetics, your habits & by your thinking.

Japanese people have developed it as an art, they call it `***Ikigai***`. Okinawans, residents of the island Okinawa, where people live for many years after becoming a hundred-year-old, have been extensively studied by scientists. The key to their longevity was found to be their diet, exercise & lifestyle. Their diet is rich in vegetables and in herbs, seaweeds, sweet potato, green tea. They eat much less salt & sugar than the other Japanese. They regularly walk long distances. They have a firm faith that everybody has a purpose in life, it is called their Ikigai, and they are busy finding a strong purpose for life. They are busy forming strong social ties, both in friends & family. They connect with nature every day. All these have a positive effect on their neurochemical balance.

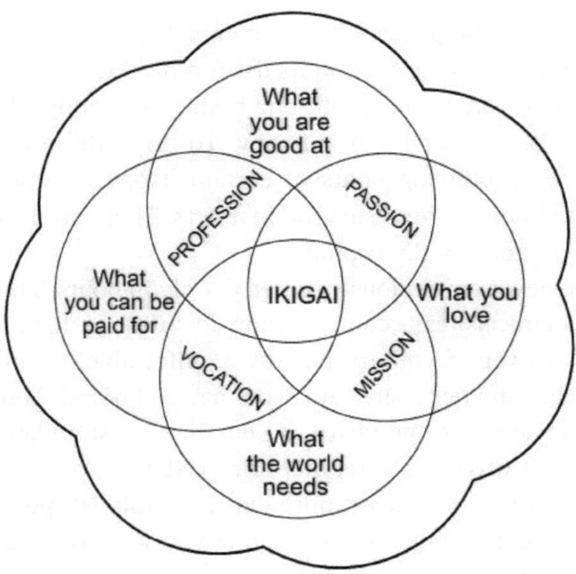

Enter Caption

Happy Chemicals

See, basically we are mammals. We have our old reptilian brain, which is concerned mainly with the regulation of the Autonomic Nervous System (ANS) with its two main branches, SNS & PSNS. With the evolving mammalian brain, we evolved our ANS and developed the polyvagal part of PSNS. The reptilian brain responded to stress by SNS, when danger was at the doorstep, it would activate of PSNS that paralyzed the animal (freeze), reptiles even feign death.

With the evolution of the mammalian brain and its polyvagal connections, social networking was established. When there was no stress, this social networking came to be used for other purposes also.

What were they?

Survival is the top priority in our mammalian brain.

Therefore, food is the first on its list & reproduction is the next. When we have eaten to our fill, our brains are happy. When we pass on our genes, our brain is happy. To bribe these behaviors, nature started producing bouts of certain happy chemicals each time we acted on, for these survival instincts. These are Dopamine, Serotonin, Oxytocin & Endorphins.

They are never continuously secreted; only in bouts. The release of these chemicals can control your feelings of happiness or unhappiness. Even if you are healthy, comfortable, economically sound & stable, in your spare time, you may feel bored. You are not at ease, you want some good stress - eustress- to stimulate you, to produce some Cortisol & Norepinephrine (NE).

By itself cortisol produces more glucose while NE pumps your heart. So you enter some competition & feel you are an achiever, successful, etc. But then, when nature won't release happy chemicals, again you feel empty. So the other parts of the brain began searching for what similar actions of reproductive success can be mimicked in social networking to simulate & therefore deceive mother nature into producing bursts of happy chemicals!

Philosophers who had no idea of neurobiochemistry had naturally come to conclusions like, "Happiness is like a butterfly. If you pursue it, it always runs ahead of you but if you stop pursuing it, stay silent and calm, the chances of that butterfly landing on you will probably increase."

The reproductive success depends upon your health, your attractiveness, choosing an appropriate mate, (all mammals by instinct avoid inbreeding as if they know that it damages DNA.), chasing out other competitors, (some mammals kill even their male off-springs), having successful reproductive behavior, then nursing, nurturing, raising the progeny, till it enters the world to ensure propagation. All these are activities nature rewards with bursts of happy chemicals.

But chemicals also find their way to other circuits, become ingrained or incorporated into certain relaxing activities & hence we can get a chance to build newer circuits that will release these happy chemicals. Some brains become expert in producing Dopamine while some become experts in producing Endorphins

Let us briefly review them so you will identify who you are - a dopamine man or Endorphin girl? One particular chemical is your neurological favorite; identify it, enhance it & start developing circuits for other happy chemicals. It is something like relishing an Indian thali. You will have your main select dish & also use side dishes like chutney, achar, papad, etc. Even though the spices are in small quantity, they will give you more delight, isn't it? We often say experiencing falling in love is happiness. And sex is just a small part of love.

Love, in fact, is the sober name of reproductive success. Love is a cocktail of many chemicals. But the subconscious attachment to it is so powerful that many spiritual sects, tantriks, etc do bring in Madhura bhakti, shakti upasana into some secret practices. Gospel of Philip (found in the 1940s; as Nag Hammadi Library) uses allogary of Bridal chamber as ultimate union with God.

Dopamineis stimulated by `Chase` aspect of love, the joy of courting. Dopamine signals to the brain that a need is about to be met. In nonreproductive circuits it got associated with planning, executing & becoming happy when you succeed. If you are a dopamine person, nurture these qualities, it is your main course. If you are not a dopamine person try developing them. It will be your spice.

Oxytocinis stimulated by touch & trust. Everything from holding hands to 'Jadooki zhappy' (Munnabhai fame Sanjubaba, yes, the same) is Oxytocin-based. Deep & intimate friendships are therefore very important. Sex, childbirth release huge amounts of oxytocin. It is a bonding hormone or cuddle chemical. Therefore, incorporate touch. We shy away from physical contacts. Make them safely.

Serotoninis stimulated by the status aspect of love - the pride of getting associated with a person of higher status. When you get respect, awards, felicitations, etc., Serotonin is released. Use your intelligence, sincerity, efforts to collect awards, certificates of which you will be proud.

Endorphins are stimulated by physical pain, by laughing & crying in love and also by a good amount of exercise. You feel endorphin release when you do sacrifices, for family, friends, or even stranger. When you share somebody else's burden, express empathy to somebody's hardships, Endorphin is released.

Cortisolis not a happy hormone, but when you lose your love, you feel bad. That bad feeling is due to Cortisol. But Cortisol makes you guard your family. It helps you recover from breakups. It's a stress hormone and though helpful in emergency, in the long run, it can cause harm.

Love feels good because it helps you keep your DNA alive in the form of future generation. But there is no free love in nature. Good feelings are a reward for the hard work done to achieve love. Bad feelings are associated when you find no possibility of love.

Something as trivial as failing to get a smile from the person you are smiling at can trigger neurochemistry so wildly, you can't even imagine. So, in short, if you study and cultivate these qualities in your life, you will be cultivating the 'Happy Chemicals'. They will improve your health, make your friendships more deep & lasting, you will take proper care of your family, you will become stress hardy & your life will become a satisfying experience.

Life moves in two planes, one is horizontal and the other is vertical. When you exercise intelligence, discrimination, value-based behaviours, you are in a logical, mathematical, horizontal plane. But you move in the same plane. Once in a while, you experience the illogical, magical side of life which manifests as serendipity or synchronicities. You are moved to a higher plane. This movement would not have been possible through your volition, rationalization, logic, etc. In fact, it is said that the most important decisions in your life are taken by coincidence, by chance.

Life literally pushes you to a higher plane & leaves you there to work with your rational logical, approach. Have you ever thought about this? Find out all major turning points in your life, major life events. Can you identify any coincidences behind them? Life is both, logical & illogical, rational & irrational. There is a time for everything, but the balance has to be taken care of. This is the happiness of moment-to-moment awareness. Out of this perception comes gratitude & gratitude is the foundation for developing habits of happiness.

CHAPTER NINE

Cognitive Behavioural Therapy (CBT)

What is CBT

Dear friends, till now we saw what is stress. This is a fact, that life is stressful & the body's natural stress response is getting overstimulated. We are carrying on this burden of stress response unabatedly. Chronic stress causes elevation of cortisol causing hyperglycemia. The elevation of norepinephrine causes cardiovascular hyperresponsiveness. Chronic stress also alters immune response and a state of chronic inflammation is activated. Markers of inflammation (CRP, TNF, 1L6) are elevated in both depression & diabetes. Thus there is a chronic inflammatory state going on in our bodies.

We know chronic inflammation is the common denominator for the epidemic of our current diseases ie. obesity, depression, diabetes, cancers, immune alterations, arthritis, GI problems, respiratory problems & even dementia. Understanding stress response & following a lifestyle that will reduce stress is no doubt an important step we can take, but one more important modality which definitely helps to reduce the impact of stress on your mental health is Cognitive Behaviour Therapy (CBT). There are many forms & variations of their basic therapy. It is mainly in the domain of clinical psychologists & psychiatrists.

The basic premise in CBT is that we are raised or rather molded by our parents, our societies, our conditionings. This occurs usually in our hypnotizable years of life (up to 7 years or so). By that time we form 'core' beliefs about life. We never question our beliefs. These beliefs are in the format - I cannot, I should not, I am inadequate; It is not good to; It is my duty to, etc. So many negative & limiting beliefs are formed in our mind, our subconscious mind, about which we are unaware of. These beliefs govern our thinking patterns, our emotions & thus affect our behavior.

The good part of this story is that these beliefs can be brought to the light of consciousness, re-examined, reframed, restructured & reformed. CBT-based therapies are done with professionals.

CBT-based therapies, when combined with stress reduction strategies & exercises, do give a very good clinical response in depression, Anxiety, Panic disorders, SAD & PTSD. But you need not wait for these disorders to afflict you. Be proactive and start relaxation techniques, breathing exercises & meditation from today only.

Since the 1990s, psychologists started investigating Happiness or wellbeing. This is an important & welcome step because life's ultimate goal is to be happy, to be useful, to be able to contribute to society; to be able to make a difference.

Traditionally, happiness is defined by two aspects.

1) Happiness based on pleasure- This is happiness derived from sensory pleasure from moment to moment. Its proponent is Indian Rishi Charvak. This happiness is dependent on senses, is short-lasting; it is wine, women & song.

There is nothing wrong in it as long as you are not harming or hurting anybody else. But it does not give any lasting satisfaction & in the end, you feel empty.

2) The second type of happiness is found in doing what is worth doing, not necessarily in having a good time. The happiness we gain from having a meaning & purpose in our lives, fulfilling our potential & feeling that we are part of something bigger than personal hardships & efforts over a long time.

This happiness is long-lasting & gives us deep contentment. If happiness is the ultimate clue to subjective well-being (SWB) then it is expressed in a formula.

SWB = Satisfaction with life + positive emotions - negative emotions.

Different questionaries are available to judge your level of satisfaction & the positive and negative emotions playing in your life. You can get an idea about SWB & also know what you need to do to improve it. Martin Seligman, one of the founding fathers of positive psychology, describes his new theory of well-being in his book 'Flourish'.

His model is called the **PREMA model**

Positive emotions are your uplifting mood. Engagement or flow is well-being you get from total absorption in the task at hand where you forget the passage of time.

Relationship- good, caring & supportive interpersonal connections are essential for well-being. The purpose or meaning of life is important because it provides both a stable foundation & a sense of direction in life.

Pursuing **meaningful activities**is more strongly related to happiness than pursuing pleasurable activities.

Accomplishment- includes everything from achievement, success & mastery at the highest possible level to progress towards goals & competence.

So - always be aware of this star of well-being & happiness & try to achieve balance in all these activities. This is the practice of positive psychology & is much more than just detoxifying the bad effects of stress on the body & mind.

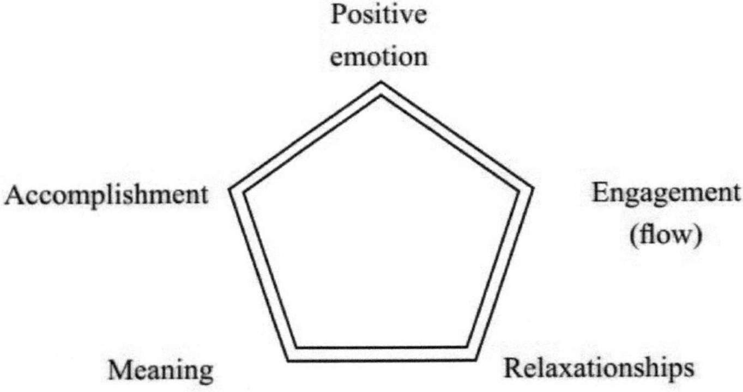

Enter Caption

Epilogue

Dear reader, you have just read this short manual on how stress is killing us and how we can save ourselves.

Spread this message to your family & friends.

All of us can be proactive and take charge of our life.

If we pass on this knowledge to our next generation, that will be a life-saving gift to them.

I express my thanks to many scientists who worked on stress and many masters who elaborated meditation.

I have freely used sources from the internet, from different authors.

I express my gratitude to all these stalwarts.

I have no copyright on this material and I wish you all should use this material freely without changing its content or format. You can copy, quote, reprint, share or gift this material to anybody who needs it.

With love to you all,

Dr. M. H. Patwardhan.

About The Author

Dr. Milind H. Patwardhan

Dr. M H Patwardhan is one of the most leading practicing endocrinologists in western Maharashtra. He completed his post-graduation and super specialization in Endocrinology from PGI, Chandigarh, one of the most prestigious and reputed institutes of all times.

He started Endocrine & Diabetes Research Center in Miraj Maharashta 1987. While working with patients suffering from all forms of Diabetes, he was moved by the lack of awareness and ignorance amongst the population regarding this disease, and founded the Madhumeh Jagruti Manch, a platform solely dedicated to patient education. He is also the editor of Madhusakha, a monthly magazine for patient education

He is also the author of Madhumeh : tantra & mantra prashna Manjusha – a simplified book that answers all commonly raised questions about Diabetes..

As an endocrinologist while studying hormonal responses to stress, Dr Patwardhan started linking it to chronic stressful situations of modern urban milieu, which is experiencing a steep & steady rise in diseases of westernization, urbanization. India has earned the status of being the Capital of Diabetes, metabolic syndrome and premature ischemic heart diseases. Interestingly , he observed that teaching how to tackle stressful situations helps patients to control diabetes and metabolic diseases.

This has become a major activity in his metabolic clinic for the past decade.

This book is one of his many efforts to help patients and population in general become aware of their own bodies, the diseases and how exactly to relieve the stress that is the root cause of everything.

Printed by Libri Plureos GmbH in Hamburg,
Germany